Why Me Lord?

Len North

New Wine Press

New Wine Press
PO Box 17
Chichester
West Sussex
PO20 6YB
England

Unless otherwise stated, all scriptures are taken from the NIV,
The Holy Bible, New International Version © copyright 1973, 1978,
1984, by The International Bible Society. Used by permission.

Additional scriptures quoted are from the AV, Authorised Version.
Crown copyright.

ISBN: 1 874367 47 7

Typeset by CRB Associates, Lenwade, Norwich
Printed in England by Clays Ltd, St Ives plc

Dedication

I dedicate this book to my wife Margaret, who introduced me to the Lord Jesus Christ as my own personal Saviour, then was bold enough to marry me. I thank her for all her help, support and encouragement during my forty years of ministry.

My thanks also to my daughter-in-law Diane, my friends Christine, Caroline, Kevin and Glyn for all their help in typing out my notes.

My purpose in writing this was to leave something behind for my grandchildren, but I pray that many others will be blessed in reading it.

Contents

	Foreword	7
	Introduction	9
Chapter 1	Evangelism as a Life Style	13
Chapter 2	You Must Have a Personal Conviction	17
Chapter 3	Let the Holy Spirit Use You	21
Chapter 4	Learn to Handle the Word of God	25
Chapter 5	Prayer Power	29
Chapter 6	Love for Lost Souls	33
Chapter 7	Practicalities	37
Chapter 8	The Early Years	43
Chapter 9	A Teenager at Last	53
Chapter 10	Service Life	57
Chapter 11	Called Into the Kingdom of God	63
Chapter 12	Called Into Service for God	69
Chapter 13	Our God is Able	73
Chapter 14	A New Life at Sixty	85

Foreword

This book gives a real insight into the challenges of English culture for the gospel in the last half-century. It gives us an idea of how faithful men and women have endeavoured to bring the claims of Christ to generations in difficult times.

Len explains in a very personal and real way how the Lord has blessed and led him through these days with a sense of personal growth in the whole wider picture.

The stories of God's goodness in provision and power are both stimulating and securing.

This book is one which will give insight and no doubt a sense of excitement of what the Lord is doing in our day right now. For these are days of new opportunity and of expansion which Len himself has experienced and explains with such clarity in the later part of his own pilgrimage.

I would suggest you read it with a sense of thankfulness for what God has done through faithful saints in previous decades and with a sense of rejoicing and expectation of what the Lord is doing amongst us all today.

Tony Morton
1996

Introduction

Evangelism Today

I have spent some forty years of my life in evangelism of one kind or another, and I want to share some of my thoughts on this subject.

Of course, we have to decide what we mean by evangelism. There are so many different kinds – mass evangelism, team witness, one night rallies, house meetings, open-air witness – the list goes on. I am more and more convinced that we need to teach the people in our churches the need for personal witness.

Someone said, 'evangelism is telling one beggar where another beggar can find bread.'

There was a time in the early 1960s when we lived and worked in Wiltshire. I had a Gospel tent in those days, and I had arrived home after being away for a time. I found my lawn filled with gypsy women and about nine or ten of their children, drinking tea and eating jam sandwiches. I ran inside to Margaret asking her, 'What's going on here? Are you holding a gypsy mission, or opening a free meals service for them?'

Margaret told me that a week before one of them had called selling pegs and had asked if the child with her could have a drink. Margaret being Margaret, not only gave the child a drink, but made mother a cup of tea and gave them both a jam sandwich. So the word had gone around that this was the place to call. I have been told that gypsies leave a mark for each other and I don't know if it's true, but the lesson is a clear one. One gypsy tells another gypsy where to find jam sandwiches!

Don't you just long for someone to call at your door asking for the 'Bread of Life'? I certainly do. Although I have knocked on hundreds of doors over the last forty years, I long for the day when the Spirit of God moves so that people actually seek for the Lord.

I don't believe we have ever lived in such days of great opportunities. People are willing and ready to talk about their faith. I always carry a booklet or tract, and seek to tell them about the need for a faith in the living Jesus who died for them. I have been privileged to introduce Jesus to people in cafés, buses and trains, in the street, and many other places. I always seek to remember that Jesus said *'Go into all the world and preach the good news to all creation'* (Mark 16:15). I don't think He meant only on a Sunday from the pulpit. I found a notice last week which read 'The Gospel will be preached here next Sunday at 6.30 pm'.

I have often been asked why we should go to the people at all, when they'll come to church if they feel the need. I do believe that people turn to Christ when they have a need, but I also believe Paul in Romans 10 when he asks *'How can they believe if they have not heard?'*

Today we live in a time when many young people don't know the name of Jesus, or if they do it is used as a swear word. So the question arises of how we reach people in this day and age? Nothing changes. People are still the same today as ever they were. Without God, and therefore without hope (Ephesians 2:12).

I believe therefore, that evangelism starts with every born-again Christian. I have spent the best part of thirty years in so-called full-time Christian service, and the more I think about it, the more convinced I am that every

Christian is in full-time service, if we are to believe 2 Corinthians 3:2 which says *'You yourselves are letters written in our hearts, known and read by everyone.'* The moment you confess Jesus as Lord, people watch you and read you, and you become their image of Christ. When they see you now, they see Him. What a great responsibility we have. How often we let the Lord down, and consequently we let people down. So many times over the years I have heard it said about various people 'If that is Christianity, I'm not interested.'

Dear people, He has no voice but yours, no hands but yours, no feet but yours in the world. Let the Holy Spirit fill you and use you to the glory of God, and the blessing of the world.

Chapter 1

Evangelism as a Life Style

All too often we get uptight and tension builds up the moment someone mentions evangelism, but you are doing it all the time. If only we could be more relaxed about our faith and give the impression that we are enjoying it, not enduring it. Maybe we take Matthew 24:13 (AV) too literally,

> 'He that shall **endure** unto the end, the same shall be saved.'

I wonder why we feel we must do something hard when we try to witness, so forgetting common-sense and becoming insensitive to people's feelings and needs? We don't need to start with Romans 3:23 every time.

> 'For all have sinned and fall short of the glory of God.'

That follows later when you have won their confidence and trust.

Look at Jesus at work with the Samaritan woman in John chapter four. We notice that He established **the contact** (verses 4–7), then guided **the conversation** (verse 10), until He had won her **confidence** (verse 10). 'Sir give me to drink' (verse 15): she is now beginning to understand that He is talking about something different from natural water, and it is then that He brings out her **conviction** (verses 16–26). Then and only then, we see her full **confession** of faith (verse 29), *'Could this be the Christ?'*

The result of that one woman's confession was that many believed (verse 39). In His humanity she could see the deity. Remember that God sent a man to show men the way. Jesus was the great communicator of God's message.

He talked with prostitutes, hugged the lepers and gave sight to the blind. His love was extravagant, and at times almost reckless.

When someone comes to Christ it is like dropping a pebble in a brook. The ripples go outwards, and you never know what God is going to do through that person.

Some time ago a man in an office witnessed to his friend who became a Christian. Since that day most of his family have come to Christ. I know that for a fact, because only last year I had the privilege of leading grandma aged 78 to Jesus, and the blessing goes on both inside the family and among many of their friends outside the family.

As a result of one man's witness I have been privileged to travel to Italy several times and have seen signs following the preaching of the Word. But I never forget that one man's witness has brought blessing to many others.

Why not start today, just where God has placed you? You may not feel you have the gift of an evangelist, but He has called you just where you are to be a witness for Him (Acts 1:8).

'Not by might nor by power, but by my Spirit, says the Lord Almighty.' (Zechariah 4:6)

Just look for the opportunity, use it and leave the rest to God. We are not told to convert the world; that's the Holy Spirit's business, but we are told to witness to the life-changing power of the Gospel. What a message you have to tell about Jesus.

I have set out a few thoughts that I believe will help you

in your witness for God; in fact I consider them to be essentials in our witness if we are to be effective for Jesus.

All too often, people desire to witness and yet don't know where to start. I trust what I have to say will lead you on to be all you desire to be, and as you go forward you will rejoice in what He has done for you.

Chapter 2

You Must Have a
Personal Conviction

It is impossible to witness for Jesus unless you know **Him** for yourself, not just having a 'head experience', but a 'heart experience' of *His saving grace*. I have often been heard to say 'One ounce of experience is worth one ton of argument' (2 Timothy 2:23–25). It isn't possible to argue anyone into the Kingdom, because if it was, you can be sure that someone much more learned than you could argue them out of the Kingdom.

Personally, I will never get into an argument about religion, but I will talk about Jesus. Whenever the Jehovah Witnesses call at my door, I tell them that I am a born-again Christian and politely shut the door; yet I rejoice to say that I have seen some Jehovah Witnesses come to the truth and later come to Jesus. I was pleased to know the power of Gospel preaching, working in their lives.

The question I must ask you is 'Do you know Jesus as your own personal Saviour?' I hope you do, if not, the answer is to start at the beginning and come to **Him** right now, wherever you are. **He** is waiting for your personal commitment. Remember **He** committed **His** life to the Cross for **You**.

Having made that start, you can now say with Paul in 2 Timothy 1:12:

> *'I am not ashamed because I know whom I have believed.'*

When we believe like that, you can't stop talking about **Him**, it's like falling in love. Remember that day? He or she filled your whole life so much you just wanted to tell the whole world. In the same way, go and tell about Jesus!

John 3:11 says:

> *'We speak of what we know and testify of what we have seen.'*

If you are feeling weak like me, why not do what I often do and read 1 Corinthians 1:26–2:5. As I have already said, don't try to be an evangelist, but be honest and sincere because in a court of law, a witness is not asked what they think, only what they know.

This doesn't mean when we come to Christ we lose our brains! Take time to look up and read 1 Peter 3:15:

> *'Always be prepared to give an answer to everyone who asks you to give a reason for the hope you have.'*

I believe one of the traps of Satan is to get us into too much activity so that we do not have the time for prayer, or reading the Word. I speak from experience here because there was a time in my life when I became what I call 'a public success but a private failure.' I got so busy for God that I almost forgot who I was serving and I had to learn the difference between honest activity and spiritual growth. I saw it was possible to suffer spiritual poverty in the midst of spiritual activity.

The Christian life is like the married life, it has to be constantly worked at. How easy it is to take our partner for granted. They are always there when we need them; so much so they become a part of us. Isn't that true about Jesus? He is always there especially when we need Him.

He too becomes part of our lives, Yet He had to say to the church at Ephesus in Revelation 2:4:

> *'You have forsaken your first love.'*

We find the great apostle Paul saying after over thirty years of service for his Lord *'I want to know Christ'* (Philippians 3:10). I love the New English Bible version of that same verse: *'All I care for is to know Christ.'* Is that how you feel about Jesus? I tell you from over forty years of experience that this relationship has to be cultivated daily, if you are to witness for **Him** and about **Him**.

Chapter 3

Let the Holy Spirit Use You

As I start this chapter I am quite conscious that many Christians have different thoughts regarding the Holy Spirit. I would be less than honest if I didn't write my own convictions and support them with experiences of my own.

Jesus said in John 3:6:

> *'Flesh gives birth to flesh, but the Spirit gives birth to the spirit.'*

Therefore, when we are born-again, it is of the Holy Spirit. Look up and read the following Scriptures: John 14:15–16; 16:13–15.

Why then do we find such a lack of power all too often in our personal witness? After all, Jesus did say in Acts 1:8:

> *'You will receive **power** when the Holy Spirit comes on you, and you will be my witnesses . . .'*

Of course I know that at that time He was talking to the disciples, yet I honestly believe that it is the same for us today, in our Jerusalem, at home; in our Judea, our town; and in our Samaria, our country; yet He goes on to say in the same verse '. . . *to the ends of the Earth.'*

I believe there are two reasons for this lack of power within many of our churches and people, and I would like to highlight them as follows.

Firstly, I have come to realise the need for the baptism of the Holy Spirit if we are to use the gifts the God has given us. Of course, this has been mis-used over the years with great emphasis on the gift of tongues, often at the expense of the other eight gifts.

I have not forgotten the nine fruits of the Spirit in Galatians 5:22. They are something that every Christian should seek to cultivate and grow in their Christian life. I am talking about the nine gifts of the Spirit in 1 Corinthians 12:7-11. Didn't Jesus say in Luke 11:13:

> *'Father in heaven will give the Holy Spirit to those who ask Him.'*

For years I knew the baptism of the Holy Spirit but didn't move in the gifts as I should because in my early years, I had a real hang-up. This was because of some over-zealous Christians telling me I couldn't be baptised in the Holy Spirit if I didn't speak in tongues, and yet in my evangelism, I was seeing many saved. Praise God I speak in tongues now, but I'm also moving in the other gifts. I'm not saying that tongues are not important, but we must get them in perspective in relationship to the other gifts.

Now I come to my second point regarding the lack of power in so many of our lives. I believe that there is one filling, but **many** anointings:

> *'Be filled with the Spirit.'* (Ephesians 5:18)

God can only fill up an empty vessel. Let me use an illustration to make this point clear.

I remember going to the seaside years ago with the children. My daughter kept bringing a bucket of water and pouring it over my feet. On one of her visits she said 'I have a bucketful Daddy,' but when she tipped it out it was half full of sand. Isn't that like us today? Something comes in to fill our lives and there isn't any room for all that the

Holy Spirit is longing to do, and so we lose our freedom of witness.

Let me just name a few of these things. I personally find that **pride** is a big enemy. Satan all too often lets us slip into this one, especially if we have had a good meeting or known blessing. We can even become proud of being humble.

Jealousy is another thing Satan uses to stop us from being blessed. Wishing I had some other person's gifts for example. You can enlarge on this one in your own mind, but I'm sure you can think of many different reasons for jealousy.

Then there is that **unforgiving spirit**. I can remember going to a church for a ten-day mission years ago. The first weekend was so hard; in fact it was so bad that I called all the members together and told them that if they didn't put right whatever was wrong, I was on my way home to my family. A woman then got up and turned to another member and said 'Sorry.'

That was the first time that they had spoken in a long time. The result was that the following night, God moved in a mighty way and several people came to the Lord in that village during the next eight days. I can't recall the numbers of those saved, but I can say that it was one of the most outstanding missions I ever held.

Then there are **wrong relationships**. Over the years I have seen so many promising young Christians led away because of wrong relationships. Always remember that Jesus said in John 15:19:

> *'You do not belong to the World, but I have chosen you out of the World.'*

We would do well to read 1 John 2:15–17 often. Yes, I know we still live in the world but remember 2 Corinthians 3:2:

> *'We are letters known and read by everyone.'*

The question we must ask ourselves is how far are we to identify ourselves with the world? What do we mean by the Holy Spirit? We must be different, but not isolated.

The Holy Spirit can only use a **holy life**. I can hear someone saying to themselves, 'He works in spite of us.' That is quite true in one sense, but He is still the Holy Spirit and all too often we Christians lower our standards to fit in with our situations. When someone in the office tells that sick joke, do we laugh or turn away? It is so easy to seek to be popular when we should be seeking to be holy. After all, didn't Jesus say in John 15:18–19:

> *'If the world hates you, keep in mind that it hated me first.'*

Now I'm not saying that we should go out of our way to be difficult, just different! Always keep in mind 1 Corinthians 6:19–20 – look it up, read it and **live by it**.

Since the day of my conversion so much has changed. I wouldn't want to go back to the bondage of those early days, but I feel we are mis-using our new found freedom. Please don't think I am being a killjoy. We are told in 1 Corinthians 8:9:

> *'Be careful however that the exercise of your freedom does not become a stumbling block to the weak.'*

I'm sure the world expects far more from Christians than the standard that many Christians live by.

> *'Do not grieve the Holy Spirit of God with whom you were sealed for the day of redemption.'*
>
> (Ephesians 4:30)

Chapter 4

Learn to Handle the Word of God

God does and will use your personal testimony, but only use it as an introduction to the Gospel. A personal testimony often leads to the opportunity to show people what God has to say from the Word.

I am a little concerned today as I watch many Christians seeking to counsel people to Christ having left their Bibles at home. After all, it is not what you think, but it is what God has to say on the matter that counts. I always find that the Holy Spirit leads me to an appropriate scripture to fit the need. The Bible has the answer to their need in Christ, therefore, as I counsel, I always say, 'Let us see what God has to say about this,' and then turn to the Word.

I was reading only last week in one of our daily papers the reason why the reporter felt that people were drifting away from the churches. He spoke of pulpit 'trendies'; those who preach a social gospel. He gave a list of figures of different denominations that were falling away, saying that in many independent churches, the membership was growing at a rate of over 100,000 every year.

I quote from the reporter:

'A major factor is the main churches' promotion of social affairs at the expense of traditional biblical teachings.'

I have to agree with him. Of course we should be involved in social affairs, yet at the same time we need to get back to biblical preaching.

Personally, I often go back to 1 Corinthians 1:26–2:5:

> *'Brothers, think of what you were when you were called. Not many of you were wise by human standards; not many were influential; not many were of noble birth. But God chose the weak things of the world to shame the strong. He chose the lowly things of this world and the despised things – and the things that are not – to nullify the things that are, so that no-one may boast before him. It is because of him that you are in Christ Jesus, who has become for us wisdom from God – that is, our righteousness, holiness and redemption. Therefore, as it is written: "Let him who boasts boast in the Lord."*
>
> *When I came to you, brothers, I did not come with eloquence or superior wisdom as I proclaimed to you the testimony about God. For I resolved to know nothing while I was with you except Jesus Christ and him crucified. I came to you in weakness and fear, and with much trembling. My message and my preaching were not with wise and persuasive words, but with a demonstration of the Spirit's power, so that your faith might not rest on men's wisdom, but on God's power.'*

When you read it through, and ask the Holy Spirit to speak to you from it. After all, Paul says in Romans 10:17:

> *'Faith comes from hearing, and hearing by the Word of God.'*

One of my great regrets is that I was not able to go to Bible college. I had little or no education when I was converted in my late twenties, but I am so pleased that the Holy Spirit gave me a tremendous thirst for the Word of

God. I would spend hours reading the Bible and also took correspondence courses. In fact, I did everything that I could to learn. Now I'm settled, I still find I have lots of time to read the Word, and after over forty years, it is still as fresh today as it was in those early days.

I love Paul's charge to young Timothy in 2 Timothy 3:10–4:8. Paul tells him to learn it; preach it; use it; that he might be thoroughly equipped for every good work. I would say to any young people reading this, if you desire to be used in evangelism, set time aside daily to read God's Word and learn it so that God can use it through you. I know He can and will. You'll find as you study it, it will be there in your mind and one day just when it's needed, God will bring it out. Of course, He can't do this if you don't study!

Let's ask ourselves why it is important to know the Word. What does it have to say about itself? As I have already said, you can never win people to Christ by argument. It's only by the **power** of the Word of God, used by the Holy Spirit of God that brings conviction and conversion. Of course there are a few exceptions, but on the whole I have proved this to be true.

Remember, the Bible is no ordinary book. I quote from the Coronation Service:

'We present you with this book, the most valuable thing this world affords, here is wisdom, this is the Royal Law, these are the live oracles of God.'

Paul tells Timothy:

'They are able to make you wise unto salvation ... for all scripture is God-breathed.'   (2 Timothy 3:15–16)

Peter tells us:

'Men spoke from God as they were moved by the Holy Spirit.'   (2 Peter 1:20–21)

The writer to the Hebrews says:

> *'For the Word of God is living and active.'*
>
> (Hebrews 4:12)

and in Ephesians 6:7 it is called *'the sword of the Spirit.'*

Not only is it inspired and instructive, it is the instrument the Holy Spirit uses in your hand in bringing a soul into a **new birth**. Imagine a gynaecologist at a difficult birth if he couldn't find the necessary instruments he needed. This is why I am saying it is important to be familiar with the Word.

I close this chapter by leaving you to read the charge God gave to Joshua in Joshua 1:6–9.

> *'Be strong and courageous, because you will lead these people to inherit the land I swore to their forefathers to give them. Be strong and very courageous. Be careful to obey all the law my servant Moses gave you; do not turn from it to the right or to the left, that you may be successful wherever you go. Do not let this Book of the Law depart from your mouth; meditate on it day and night, so that you may be careful to do everything written in it. Then you will be prosperous and successful. Have I not commanded you? Be strong and courageous. Do not be terrified; do not be discouraged, for the Lord your God will be with you wherever you go.'*

Also 2 Timothy 2:15:

> *'Study to show thyself approved unto God a workman that needeth not to be ashamed, rightly dividing the Word of Truth.'*

Chapter 5

Prayer Power

This is now getting down to the hard part, because I'm sure that like me, you don't find prayer easy. So often when we set time aside, we can think of one hundred and one other things we want to do instead. Satan reminds us of the cleaning and other things we need to do today, so we find it difficult to give our minds wholly to prayer.

I am totally convinced that prayer is the **power house** of all our Christian service; we have to learn that we have to **go to God for sinners** before we ever **go to sinners for God**.

We so often get into a routine in our praying that we can recognise some Christians by the prayers they pray. I have been to many church meetings, knowing who was going to pray and what they were going to pray for. They would pray what I call 'bus stop' prayers; picking someone up and dropping them off and on to the next person. This is not praying, but simply just saying prayers. Please don't think that I am sounding too critical because I too often fall into this trap.

Paul tells us:

> *'In everything by prayer and petition with thanksgiving, present your requests to God.'*　　　(Philippians 4:6)

Likewise, 1 Thessalonians 5:17 tells us to *'pray continually'*.

Personally, I'm not too sure if God is impressed by long prayers (of course there are times for these!), but in relation to our personal witness, it is often more beneficial to send up short, sharp prayers for the person you are witnessing to at that moment. How often I have cried 'Lord, help me' and He has.

There are times when we need to spend time in prayer and fasting for the world in which we live, and for the people we meet with daily. Didn't Jesus say:

> *'The harvest is plentiful, but the workers are few, ask the Lord of the harvest to send workers into the harvest fields.'* (Matthew 9:37–38)

Look up and read the story of the boy with the evil spirit (Mark 9:14–32). In verse 29 Jesus tells His disciples:

> *'This kind can come out only by prayer and fasting.'*

I have seen people delivered from evil spirits and I say from experience that it they don't always leave easily. Yet Jesus has given us the authority:

> *'And these signs will accompany those who believe, in **my name** they will drive out demons.'* (Mark 16:17)

It is by claiming the truth of the Word of God, supported by prayer (see Matthew 18:18–20) and then acting upon what you believe. Of course, you may get it wrong, but don't let that stop you. After all, a person who never makes a mistake never makes anything. If you do get things wrong, just admit you've got it wrong and trust God to help you the next time. Read what James 4:3 has to say:

> *'When you ask, you do not receive because you ask with the wrong motives.'*

Personally, I am a great believer in being specific in praying for people. Ask God to lay upon your heart the person or persons He would have you pray for and see how God works in their lives. I love the story of the early church in Acts 4:22–36, especially verses 29–31. In verse 33, they knew what they wanted and went for it. Jesus teaches us much about prayer in Matthew 6:5–18. And in Matthew 7:7 He said:

'Ask, seek, knock and it will be given to you.'

In the same vein, James 4:2–3 says:

'You do not have because you do not ask God.'

Of course, James would be talking about many things in that verse, but the principle is still the same. We need to be bold in our praying. We see this in Genesis 18 when Abraham pleads for Sodom. As Christians, we should be pleading for our beloved country because I often wonder where we are going and what God is going to do about it. Outside of revival, I see no hope for this land!

I have heard it said that you can tell the strength of a church by its prayer meeting. All too often, it's the poorest attended meeting of the week. We then wonder why people are not coming to Christ and we look around for someone to blame. Mostly, we blame the leaders or Pastor.

If what I am writing does nothing else, I pray it will call people to prayer, not only at the church meeting, but to spend time alone with the Lord. Matthew 6:5–15 says a lot about prayer. Why not set your alarm 15 minutes early every day? I know God will bless you and you will become more of a blessing to others as a result.

This chapter is called 'Prayer Power' but I'm sure we have yet to see the full power of God released because His people who have been called to prayer, are not as enthusiastic in this area as the Lord would like. If you study the history of revivals, their beginnings can always be traced back to faithful prayer, often by some obscure person or persons, who remained faithful in prayer over the years.

Lay hold of God and see His power at work, not only in your life, but in the lives of those you have prayed for. Our God is able and willing, the question is, are we?

Chapter 6

Love for Lost Souls

Inspired by **love**, you'll see every soul as the one Christ died for. I always love to read the scriptures using the personal pronoun, and to be able to say with Paul *'I live by faith in the Son of God who loved **me** and gave himself for **me**'* (Galatians 2:20).

How much He loves us. It cost Him His very life on the cross. I wonder how much your Christian life is costing you. It is so easy to settle down to a cosy life forgetting the price He paid.

We need to ask for a **Father's heart of love**. Some time ago, I was on my way to hospital to visit a dear Christian friend. As I was getting dressed, I looked out of my bedroom window and saw three of my neighbours whom I had witnessed to. God spoke to my heart as I said to my wife 'If Billy lives or dies today, he is going to win.' My heart was broken before the Lord when my friend passed into glory that morning, but I shall never forget the peace I felt as I sat beside him with his wife as he passed away.

I honestly believe that any service we do for God must always be controlled by love for Him and for the world outside of Christ. Love must always be our controlling motive, or our service will become useless and ineffective.

2 Corinthians 5:14 says *'For Christ's love compels us.'* One of my favourite passages of scripture is in 1 John 4:7–21:

> *'Dear friends, let us love one another, for love comes from God. Everyone who loves has been born of God and knows God. Whoever does not love does not know God, because God is love. This is how God showed his love among us: He sent his one and only Son into the world that we might live through him. This is love: not that we loved God, but that he loved us and sent his Son as an atoning sacrifice for our sins. Dear friends, since God so loved us, we also ought to love one another. No-one has ever seen God; but if we love one another, God lives in us and his love is made complete in us.*
>
> *We know that we live in him and he in us, because he has given us of his Spirit. And we have seen and testify that the Father has sent his Son to be the Saviour of the world. If anyone acknowledges that Jesus is the Son of God, God lives in him and he in God. And so we know and rely on the love God has for us.*
>
> *God is love. Whoever lives in love lives in God, and God in him. In this way, love is made complete among us so that we will have confidence on the day of judgment, because in this world we are like him. There is no fear in love. But perfect love drives out fear, because fear has to do with punishment. The one who fears is not made perfect in love.*
>
> *We love because he first loved us. If anyone says, "I love God," yet hates his brother, he is a liar. For anyone who does not love his brother, whom he has seen, cannot love God, whom he has not seen. And he has given us this command: Whoever loves God must also love his brother.'*

Read it and let the Holy Spirit implant it within your heart.

One day during my door to door visiting, I called on a woman who was known in the neighbourhood for her coarse language, and her life style which left a lot to be desired. But as I began to tell her about Jesus she broke down and asked me what it was her Christian neighbour had that that she didn't, because she had been so impressed by the love and peace that always reached out to her.

Over a cup of coffee, I led her to Jesus. Some months afterwards, it was my privilege to see her, her husband and her family, baptised. What a change had taken place in that family, the result I believe, of the love shown by her neighbour.

I believe we can have all the attributes I have spoken about in the last five chapters and still not be a witness, unless we have one final thing which I would like to share with you.

The Surrender of Yourself to the Lord

Now before I start, I can hear you all saying 'but I gave myself to Him years ago,' or maybe only a short time ago. What I am trying to say is this: it is not what you hope to be, or are trying to be, but the giving of yourself daily with all your weaknesses and failings, and saying with Isaiah in chapter 6: *'Here am I, send me.'* **He said** *'Go and tell this people.'*

It's not what you say that counts, but what you are. Sad to say the world can't hear what the church has to say because of what it's doing.

To be an effective witness means to give yourself, your time, your talents, your friendship and your ambition. Read Romans 12:1–2.

You'll then find that God can and will use you for His glory and the blessing of those around you. Over the years, I have found so much help in reading 1 Corinthians 1:27–2:5. That is why I have called this book *Why Me Lord?*.

Chapter 7

Practicalities

Before I go any further, I would like you to put down this book and do a little Bible study. I know this will be helpful to you in your service to Him; be it in personal witness or door to door.

Having set out some of the questions I have often been asked, I have tried to answer them for you, but remember what I have been saying and use the Word of God whenever and wherever possible in your answers.

You don't have to preach to be a witness. Just be natural, courteous and polite, and always show love by your attitude. After all, someone, somewhere told you about Jesus. Can you remember who and when? I can, and it changed my life and attitude completely. How true Paul is in 2 Corinthians 5:17 when he says:

> 'If anyone is in Christ he is a new creation, the old has gone the new has come.'

I have been privileged to see many lives changed and it gives me a great thrill in my older years to hear from many of them today. To God be all the glory. So go for it!

Door to Door Witness

Scripture reading: Luke 10:1–12 with verse 16.
Why go to people at all, why not let them come to us? The

37

question is, how often have you been visited by a Christian? We shall never have a vision **to go** until we realise:

- **Ephesians 2:12**: Without God – without hope.
- **2 Corinthians 4:4**: The god of this age has blinded the mind of unbelievers. What then is the message we are to take? It hasn't changed.
- **Romans 1:16**: I am not ashamed of the gospel – the power of God. Men and women do not need an intellectual argument to get saved. They need to hear about Jesus. You feel weak and unable? You are in a good place.
- **1 Corinthians 2:1–5; 1 Corinthians 15:1–4**: See what Paul said. Let Jesus go with you. You are not going on a spiritual picnic, but you are engaged in a spiritual battle (Ephesians 6:10–18). Not all battles are won at the first attempt. Don't give up. Go back again if God says so.

A few practical hints to help you on your way:

1. Be natural

Try not to get uptight; be yourself. Don't feel you have to come in with a spiritual hammer every time (Romans 3:23; 6:23). Every person is different with different needs. Tell them who you are and why you have come. Seek to give them confidence in you as a person.

2. Always be courteous and polite

No foot in the door – here I am and here I stay! **Don't walk over their lawn** and **do shut the gate**. Show an interest in their children, garden and dog. Be careful not to be side-tracked. Remember what you are there for.

3. Pray that the Spirit will give you wisdom

I often go alone, but where possible, it is better to go in twos. One prays, the other talks. Seek to know where to go and when to go.

4. *Do remember you are in a spiritual battle*

Pray about where and when to go and take the Word with you. Always be prepared to give an answer (1 Peter 3:15). You are there to tell them of Jesus.

Some practical advice regarding questions you might be asked:

(a) *If God is a God of love why are there wars/famines etc.?*

– To many questions there is no answer outside of faith. I often turn them to Matthew 24:4–8; 2 Timothy 3:1–9. They can relate to this because of TV. This often leads into the second coming.

(b) *What about other religions?*

– All other leaders are dead – **Jesus is alive.**

– He said: John 14:6. He's God: John 1:1–2; Titus 2:11; Revelation 1:18, 22:18–22.

– If all else fails ask if they accept the Ten Commandments (Exodus 20:1–17).

(c) *But I don't believe in God*

– Be careful with this one, it's often a cover-up for some misdeed, or they are under conviction. I have seen many atheists pray.

– Turn them to the Word: Psalm 19:1–4; 14:1. Remember Romans 10:8–17; Hebrews 11:6.

– Remind them that Satan believes: James 2:19.

(d) *I live a good life, I'm sincere and honest etc.*

– Proverbs 16:25: There is a way that seems right but . . .

– I often ask why I have to teach my children to be good then turn them to Psalm 51:5; Isaiah 64:6; Jeremiah 17:9; Romans 3:23; 1 John 1:8; Ephesians 2:10.

– Let the Holy Spirit bring conviction. No-one ever goes to a doctor unless there is pain. No-one ever comes to Christ without conviction.

– As you are leaving, ask why they think Jesus died.

(e) *The Bible is full of contradictions*

– Give them your Bible and ask them to show you one!

- Remind them of 2 Timothy 3:16; Hebrews 4:12; 2 Peter 1:21.
- Let the Word do its own work. Leave them something behind. Always remember it is the sword of the Spirit (Ephesians 6:17–18).

(f) *There is no resurrection or hell. When you are dead, you are dead*
- Paul said 1 Corinthians 15:1–7, 500 people saw Jesus.
- Ask them if they hope to go to Heaven when they die. Many say – I hope so! Turn them to John 14. People don't like to face up to Hebrews 9:27.
- Jesus believed and talked about hell. Do deal generally with people on this one because they have often lost a loved one or been hurt regarding same.

(g) *I have always been a Christian*
- I was born one! I am British! Does being born in a stable make one a horse?
- I have made many helpful contacts by asking what they think a Christian is. Turn them to Acts 11:26 – the disciples were first called Christians; Acts 26:28 – persuade me to be a Christian; 1 Peter 4:16 – suffer as a Christian.
- To every question there is an answer! You are doing what Jesus told you to do, therefore always point them to Him.
- Mark 16: 15 – Go into all the world and preach . . .
- Acts 1:8 – You will be my witnesses.
- 2 Timothy 2:15 – Present yourself to God . . .

Remember
- **Don't** get involved in politics.
- **Don't** waste time.
- **Don't** claim to have all the answers but point them to the Word of God – it's up-to-date.

What then have we learnt from this?
- The need to go to the people.
- The need to be natural and polite.

- The need to be able to use God's Word.
- The need to be guided by the Holy Spirit.
- Remember you are not sent out to make converts, that is the Holy Spirit's ministry.
- Preach the Good News (Mark 16:15).
- Preach the Word in season and out (2 Timothy 4:2).
- Remember Jesus said: Luke 10:16; Ecclesiastes 11:1–6.

Chapter 8

The Early Years

Life began for me in August 1922 but as I had only just been born I don't remember much about it. I was just under five pounds, and I hope, the joy of my mother's heart.

My father worked for a local farmer who happened to be my uncle. Dad was his horseman and I'm told he was one of the best; able to plough a furrow straighter than most men. At that time all the work on a farm was done by men and horses with little mechanical help.

Life must have been hard for my parents. Dad worked long hours for a small wage, and we lived in a small tithe cottage in the Isle of Ely. I remember it only had two rooms with a shed in the back and no running water. The privy was in the garden, and consisted of hole in the ground, which attracted all the flies in the summer. No wonder there was so much sickness about. The farmer lived in the big house down the road.

Before I went to school my mother had two more boys, both of whom died. I clearly remember the last one because I was about four years old when he died and I was sent up the road to my aunt who told me that an aeroplane was coming to take Derek to be with Jesus. At exactly the right moment, one flew overhead. This was a great event in those days, and I ran in to my aunt to tell her that the aeroplane had come for my brother. Although

I was full of joy that Derek's suffering was now over, his death was a loss for me because I had spent hours playing with him, and now I was all alone.

Like all children I started school at the age of five, and my twin nieces who were about two years older than I was, were put in charge of me. We had over three miles to walk to school, and how far it seemed at the end of the day coming home. I was always full of all I had done at school during the day.

Not long after this my father changed his job and became a Farm Manager and we went to live in a big farmhouse. Part of it was shared by the farmer's son. Mother looked after him and as I write I can picture it now. To a small boy it seemed like a palace. It had a very large lawn with trees all around a big driveway. A gardener kept it tidy. It had cows, and chickens running about, and to my mind was everything that a farm should be.

Dad looked after the workmen, while mother made butter, picked up the eggs and did all the things a farmer's wife did. What happy times we had together looking for the eggs. I was able to drink all the milk I needed and would spend hours just playing around the farm, and watching the animals being born. Looking back, these were the happiest years of my childhood. I had everything I needed and I was so happy at that time.

As school was quite some way away we had a school bus, which was quite an event at that time. One thing that stands out in my memory about that time, is that one Sunday my teacher saw me playing with a ball in the yard, and the following day I was made to stand out in front of my class. I was made to feel the greatest sinner our side of hell. You just didn't play games on the Sabbath. Personally I feel it put folk off Christianity, but religion was a set of rules you had to obey or you were on your way to hell. How sad that so many people missed all the joy and freedom we know today that Jesus can, and will give, to those who belong to Him.

When I was about seven years old everything started to go wrong in our family. My father started to see a young lady in the village She worked on the farm and was about 18 years old. As a small boy I just couldn't understand what was happening. My mother would drag me around with her some nights trying to catch my father out. The family I had known became so different.

Father got the sack and we had to move again to a small farm cottage miles away from all the happiness I had known for the past year or so, and once again he became a farm labourer. My parents grew apart from one another and I became so insecure I was quite ill, not knowing or understanding what was happening all around me.

The cottage we moved into was down a lane, miles from anywhere. A house but no longer a home; just somewhere that people lived. The only good thing I remember about it was harvest time, and being out in the fields catching rabbits. Mother would bring the tea out for the workers, as most of the harvest was done by hand. How hard those men worked in the fields all day, cutting the corn and stacking it so that it would dry to be carried into the farm later.

Once again I had some three miles to walk to school. If we had gone by road it would have been over five miles, so we walked across the fields. On the way we had to cross a little footbridge. We would stop and play, watching the little fish swimming by. Of course one always remembers the sunny days and there seemed to be more of them at that time.

On the way home we often called in at a little cottage at the end of the lane for a cool drink. One lovely June day the old lady who lived there told me that God had sent me a little sister. I ran the next mile into the house, straight up the stairs to the bedroom and there she was; my own little sister Jean. I had never had a sister before. What joy she brought to me then, and still does today.

Three weeks afterwards, Mum, Jean and I went off to Murrow for her to be christened: by tradition, all the family went to Murrow Chapel to be christened. Dad saw us off at the station on the Friday saying he would follow the next day when he had finished his work. But he never came and I didn't see him again for nearly two years. That was in court where he was charged with desertion and sent to Bedford jail for three months, which was the law before the War. The last thing he said to me was 'See you when I come out son,' but he never came back.

My world fell down around me then. I had a wonderful mother, but how could she keep two children with no support? They did let us stay in the house for a while to see if he would come back. If he had I am sure he would have got his job back.

I can never forget sitting in Spalding workhouse while they had a committee meeting to decide if they should take us in or support us outside. Remember there was no DSS then as there is today; only the poor law. I am told they gave mother 7/6d per week ($37\frac{1}{2}$ pence) but we managed. I have often wondered how we did, but people were so kind to us and helped all they could despite their own poverty.

When the time came for Dad's return, we all went to Spalding Station to meet the train. No Dad. After waiting all day we returned home, with mum making all the excuses. But somehow I just knew in my heart that he never would again. We didn't hear anything from him for another year or so until once again he was taken to Court, and was sent to Bedford Prison for another three months. I just couldn't face it this time so I stayed at home with my auntie. I didn't see him again for nearly thirty years.

From Spalding we moved back to Murrow. Grandad had been able to find us a home in the village. It turned out to be a converted railway carriage; just two rooms, overrun with mice. In fact I spent most of my evenings catching them – sometimes catching as many as ten a night. On some occasions we even had rats visit us. What comfort! Mum was expected to pay 6/6d per week rent for this. Remember we only received 7/6d.

It wasn't long before she was behind with the rent and in debt and I shall always remember one Saturday morning when there was a knock on the door and the man said he was the bailiff and had come regarding the rent arrears. He brought an old man with him who was to live in our house for a week to make sure we didn't take anything out. I can see mum now giving him a chair and saying 'you sit there, and there you stay.' I often wonder if she gave him anything to eat, but knowing my mum I guess she did.

The following Saturday early in the morning, a van arrived to take away our home. We were left with a bed, in which all three of us had to sleep. I must say in passing they had to leave what were essentials for living.

Our furniture was taken to Wisbech market where even to this day you can take anything you want to sell to be auctioned, and there our home was sold.

We didn't know it but some of the people from the village went there to buy it back for us. Chairs were being sold for as little as 3d or 6d; I'm told the whole lot only fetched 37/6d (£1.37½p). The auctioneer of course, had to accept what was offered. You can imagine our surprise when in the afternoon a horse and wagon pulled up and most of our home was returned to us, It had been bought by the people in Murrow; mostly people from the Chapel.

My Mother couldn't get over it because she didn't go to the Chapel very often. I'm sure she had a faith in God but it was some years afterwards when she came into a living faith in our Lord Jesus Christ. How her faith must have been tested during these years, but she never seemed to be bitter, just content to bring up two small children on her own.

Life hadn't been easy for her at all; she was sent off to service in some big house at a very young age. How lonely and hard it must have been for many such country girls, working 12–15 hours a day for a very small wage as kitchen maids. She often told me stories of the old days as she called them. We would know little about it today without the stories we see on our TVs of 'Upstairs and Downstairs'.

Like so many, she returned home with an unwanted baby. Her parents were very good to her and they brought up my step-sister who I always thought was my aunty until I was old enough to understand. What a good friend my step-sister turned out to be in my later life.

During this time my mother thought that religion should play a part in my life so I was sent up the road to Murrow Methodist chapel, a lovely chapel and quite large for the size of the village. The church was at the other end of the village so the chapel was well attended. It was Sunday school in the morning, chapel Service in the afternoon and if mum wanted me out of the way it was chapel at 6 pm.

In Sunday school we were taught all the old Bible stories like David and Goliath, Daniel in the lions den and many more. An advantage for me was that my teacher was interested in my step-sister, and if he said too much to me I always told him I would tell Dulcie. I found the services most boring. One Sunday afternoon after the preacher said I should leave if I wasn't interested, I did – never to return.

One of the highlights of chapel life was the Anniversary Sunday. A platform would be built; all the girls would have pretty frocks and the boys would be in clean shirts for a change, and we would sing choruses and say our poems. I don't know why, but I always said a long one; always twenty-four line verses. I remember one particular Anniversary; I was word perfect, people came up to congratulate me, saying one day I would be a Preacher. Little did I know how true that would prove to be. Many years later I preached at one Anniversary at the Chapel.

On the following Monday it was always the Sunday School outing. We would gather at the Chapel about 2 pm and a farmer would arrive with his horses and wagons. Off we went for a ride, singing choruses and in general letting the village know it was our day. About three miles away there was another little Chapel where we all had tea and a drink and then we had the return journey to Murrow. It was great fun and it always seemed to be sunny on outing days.

I would be about 9–10 years old at the time, and today I look back with great joy to those days. It was one of the highlights of my young life. Remember there wasn't much joy in my life at that time; living in poverty in a run-down railway carriage. It made quite a change from catching mice, and we were well fed for that day of the year. The folk at the Chapel worked hard to make it a happy day for us all and we were grateful for it. The children today would think it all so unfashionable, and I guess it was, but we enjoyed it.

The only advantage of living in Murrow was that the school was only just up the road, so I had no excuse not to go, although I never did like school. Children can be, and often are, very cruel and Murrow children proved to be no exception – reminding me of things I already knew, like I was a weak little thing, and that I had no father. That was what I was growing into; a weak sickly, bitter little lad of nine or ten. I know it sounds like a sad story but that is what it was. I often cried myself to sleep because I was lonely and hungry. It always seemed that my sister came first, but after all she was seven years younger than I was and growing fast. At times she got me many a good hiding for something I hadn't done, but I really did love my baby sister, and I still do.

We were turned out of our railway carriage and became homeless yet again. The local Parish Council had some small cottages outside of the village in the middle of nowhere. They were mainly for the old but they offered us one. The rent was only 1s. (5p) per week. It was a home and had a very large garden and we were able to grow most of our own food. A farmer let us have six hens and things got a bit easier for us. I know as a lad of 10–11 I had to dig the garden. There was no running water but only a well that caught the water off the roof. If it didn't

rain we soon ran out of water and had to use it very care-
fully, and for light it was paraffin lamps or candles. From
a practical point of view we had all we needed, but it was
very damp and cold during the winter months, especially
when the money and coal ran out. Then I would spend
hours chopping wood and going around the hedgerows
looking for wood. Occasionally my brother-in-law could
let us have a few bags of logs. By this time my step-sister
had married and her husband was very good to mum.

As far as I was concerned my health wasn't very good,
and I spent some three months in an isolation hospital
with scarlet fever and diphtheria. When my family visited
me they could only look through the windows. It wasn't
easy trying to carry on a conversation through a glass
window with a lot of other people trying to do the same. I
hadn't been home long before they found I had a spot on
my lung and off I went to Norfolk and spent four months
in a sanatorium. It was very nice after I got over the three
weeks of treatment; in fact in some ways I was sorry to
leave, but of course I longed to be back with my family
again.

By this time my mother had got herself a job on the
land, working for an old man who I thought was quite
mad. Also I had to spend the rest of my childhood looking after my little sister. By this time the Secondary School
to which I should have to go was over five miles away. I
had no bike so I just didn't go; the reason given was that I
said I was ill, which all too often proved to be quite true.

At the weekends I quite often went into Wisbech to stay
with some friends. They were very kind to me and I spent
many happy hours with them. They both worked in a big
house. He did the driving/handiwork and she helped in
the house, until after a while she went off to Spalding to
visit her family and I had to sleep with him. I was about
twelve at the time and he just couldn't keep his hands
away from me. No word was ever spoken but it was a
kind of game he played at night. He was never vulgar with
me but I came to hate him and didn't want to go any

more. Mum couldn't understand why and I couldn't tell her. Maybe if I had she would have understood! In many ways it has helped me to understand why abused children feel so alone and helpless, feeling that no-one would understand or believe them.

I should say in passing that many years afterwards I went to Spalding Youth for Christ and made a point of looking for him. I hoped to say I had forgiven him and to tell him about Jesus, but when I called his family was there, so I just told them what Jesus had done for me. I am sure he knew why I had called and I have often wondered how he felt that day seeing me after so long. Maybe God was working in his heart as I spoke to them all.

We all know that abuse to children didn't stop in the period before the war. I have met so many children during my ministry with sad tales to tell. It has helped me to help them during this sadness. It seems to me that the children always blame themselves and I know that isn't true, it's just that they are afraid of the consequence regarding their families. They are afraid it will break up the family. Thank God for Childline and other organisations that are there to help.

Chapter 9

A Teenager at Last

What great expectations we have when we become a teenager. I am afraid most of my teenage years were like the rest of my life up to then.

My mother became ill and at fourteen years old I had to begin work on a farm, starting at 7 am and finishing at 5 pm, including Saturday morning, for 12/6d per week (62½p). I gave mum 10/- (50p) and had the rest for my clothing and other needs. But how I hated farming. Hoeing sugar-beet, driving a horse and cart, feeding pigs, picking potatoes. I promised myself I would get off the farm as soon as possible but there was nothing else to do in the Fens for a lad with little or no education.

The big thing for me was that at last I had some money of my own. It was only 2/6d per week but it was mine to spend as I pleased. I thought I was free at last. I found myself growing into a man, yet getting even more bitter as time went by. Life just seemed one round of work because I still had this big garden to dig and plant. I had as many responsibilities as some married men. Often when I set off in the morning with my bottle of cold tea and dripping sandwiches, I wondered where all this would end.

One good thing was growing my own strawberries and sending them off to market. I was able to make myself a little cash and that was useful because I was now able to go out with the village lads on Saturday, walking up and down the streets of Wisbech trying to date the girls.

During these days and for many years I was so insecure, and but for the grace of God I would still feel the same way. God has helped me and shown me that I am a child of the King. It took Him years to make me understand His Fatherhood and how good it is to know that our security is in **Him**. Now I can say *'Abba Father'* (Romans 8:15).

My step-sister married in 1937 and her husband became a great pal of mine. At the time of their marriage they had very little money. They lived in a farm cottage about 10 miles from where we lived, and they both worked on the farm getting their home together.

I would spend a lot of time with them during my teens. Albert and I would go out with the gun looking for a cheap dinner and often finding one. Sometimes by night we would often have to run and hide from the local copper, but that was the way of life and after all, we had to eat.

Things were very hard before the war for people living in the country. Most of us grew our own food. Albert kept a pig which he killed for meat. Life was simple and hard but somehow everyone had a satisfaction within their family which seems to be lacking today. Of course, there was no such thing as a holiday; just work and more work. If you didn't work you didn't live!

As a teenager I always longed to join the RAF. I would go to Peterborough Air Show and dream of flying and becoming someone because as I said, I just hated farm-work! But because of my lack of education I felt I had no hope. I remember going into the RAF recruiting office for all the details and coming out feeling somehow I would never make it and would have to spend the rest of my life as a farm labourer.

In 1939 the war started and I was just 17 and saw my chance of getting in. They were calling for men to join the forces but they wouldn't take me at 17 so I joined the Home Guard and became one of what is now known as

'Dad's Army'. I really enjoyed this, the training, marching and night-time mock battles. I would go off every Sunday morning for the training. I got on very well, learning how to use a gun and make petrol bombs etc. At last I was important, or was I? I don't know if we could have done much to the Germans had they come.

Just before my eighteenth birthday I tried again for the RAF. I just longed to be part of the war. How mad you can get when you are a teenager! Mum was so scared I would never get in but for three months I worked hard at the things I knew I would have to do to pass the examination, and off I went for three days to see if I was accepted or not. I had to go to the big city of London. Having never been there before you can imagine how this country boy felt. I had never seen an underground train, let alone travelled on one. How big and dirty the city seemed to me. Everyone was so busy rushing around, and it was also during the time of the Battle of Britain, so for a while I began to wish I had stayed at home after all.

For the next three days it was tests and more tests; what did I want to do and why? When I told them I wanted to fly I can see the look on the Officer's face to this day as he said to me 'What – with your eye-sight?' Anyway they accepted me. I think it was a case of you are alive and warm and we need men! So on September 9th 1940 I became 1270823 AC2 NORTH L.C. I had made it at last.

I was told to return home and I would be called up within weeks. Upon my return there was a big air-raid on London and I had to spend the night in Kings Cross Underground Station with many others. I have often thought of those folk who had to spend many nights there during the next few years. What spirit they must have had to work by day and go down there by night. Of course at that time there were many daylight raids on London.

Upon my return the first thing my mother said was 'they didn't accept you did they?' When I said yes, I guess she remembered The Great War and she didn't want to lose her own son because I just felt she thought I would never return. Praise God I did and here I am!

I was called up in a matter of weeks, sent to Blackpool for my training and soon proved what an advantage my Home Guard training was as I was often called out to show the rest of the lads how to march etc. But I am afraid in my early Service days the bitterness of the past years showed itself in my disregard to obeying orders and this resulted in getting myself into a lot of trouble. It took me a long time to learn that orders were given to be obeyed. I was a very wilful person but learnt in the end that if a man has authority over you – you obey him or suffer the consequences by doing a lot of duties when you should be out enjoying yourself with the lads: not that we had too much money to enjoy ourselves with – only 10/- (50p) per week of which I sent mum 7/6 home.

Chapter 10

Service Life

I spent six weeks in Blackpool, learning Service Drill and discipline and then I was sent to a night fighter Squadron working with the Aircrew. How I longed to fly with them, little realizing what an important part Beaufighter Bombers would play in my life later.

Yet somehow I still didn't find all I was looking for in Service life. I was the first lad in our village to join the Service and to return on leave in uniform made me feel quite proud as I walked out with RAF VR on my uniform. Still I wanted something more. It was **Jesus** I needed but I didn't realize that for the next six years.

On my return from leave they asked for men to go overseas. I was one of the first to volunteer. I must have been mad! In May – just eighteen and a half – I was put on a boat to Egypt. We didn't know where we were going or how long it would take. In fact it took over six weeks.

The convoy went out into the Ocean round the Cape by South Africa. We had seven days in port there. I only got ashore one day but how wonderful to put your feet on dry land and what a lovely place Durban proved to be. We had lost one troopship on the way, picking up 13 from that ship as it went down. By this time I wasn't feeling quite so brave after all. As we went up the Red Sea and got off the ship in Egypt, all I could see was sand and more sand. I remember saying to myself, 'Lenny boy, you will never find what you are looking for here.' It wasn't long before I found myself in the Western desert.

For nearly four years I was to be overseas going up the Western desert twice and coming out in two retreats from the desert. I can assure you that the desert is not the romantic place that films make it out to be. For the first two years we lived a very hard life, with very little water and sand, sand and more sand. Most days we were raided by German aircraft and I found myself becoming hard and bitter as time went on, with no faith in God or man. How was it that you could eat with your mate one day and bury him the next? I had no answers to the problems in my mind.

It was during this period of my life that I had a letter from a young girl. She said she was just 18 years old and had been given my address and we started to become pen pals. Apart from my family I had very little mail and often it took weeks to reach us. Mostly you received it when you returned to base camp for your two weeks rest. No wonder we all went mad on the town; with three months back pay. After being in the desert with only the 100 or so men you worked with, what a lovely sight it was to see a woman. We were usually broke after a few days.

On our last retreat I got in the way of something quite nasty and got blown up. That cost me fourteen months in hospital with two major operations on my back and lung. For the first five weeks I wasn't expected to live and at times I didn't care if I did or not.

We had been on Wellington Bombers with 108 Squadron, but now we were to be reformed because during my stay in hospital a big advance had been made and we were sent up to North Africa. How strange to drive through towns we had been bombing before and to know you had been a part of freeing them from the Germans, or that is what we thought. I wonder what the local people felt about it all. In some cases they welcomed us, in others you could feel the anger of the people; after all we were the people who had killed some of their loved ones.

In North Africa we were reformed as 39 Squadron and given Beaufighters. I was now back with the first aircraft I ever worked on and soon I was able to fulfil my ambition and fly often. It wasn't as aircrew, but we serviced the aircraft, and they always took ground crew with them when they did an air test. The pilot would take the aircraft up an if nothing fell off, the plane passed the test. This might sound like a joke but it was for real because we were working under great pressure at the time, using our aircraft to drop torpedoes on the German shipping. Often we would send out eight aircraft and if six came back it was a good day. Many who returned had been shot up. It was a sad time for us, as we were losing so many men we knew and respected.

During this time I had my 21st birthday. We were in Tunisia at the time, nowhere near the lovely places people now go for holidays. I can see myself now sitting in my tent with my one bottle of beer (our weekly ration) waiting for the return of the fellows from a raid. What a 21st!

We had moved forward into North Africa and as I was flying one day, at about 5,000 feet, the pilot called over the intercom for me to look at the starboard engine. I saw it was on fire and I became afraid. I would sooner be a live coward than a dead hero, and it looked a long way to fall. The aircraft fell out of the sky and down we went into the side of a hill. The wing came off and it burst into flames. I just felt that this was the end because as I tried to get out I found I was trapped by my legs. The pilot was able to free himself and began to chop me free. I felt that every breath was to be my last. My hair was burning, my flying coat was in flames and I cried to God to save me from this living hell, because I knew that was where I was going. I was quite godless in my way of life and outlook. But this was different. There was no-one else to call. Anyway we managed to pull ourselves out and the last I remember was stumbling on the port wing about to jump when there was a loud bang – that was all I remembered.

Some four or five days later I came to and I could hear

German voices. I was in a German Field Hospital, and we heard afterwards that some Arabs had taken us there. For the next six weeks I was reported missing, believed killed. Some three months later I was returned to my Squadron with three months back pay. I tried to forget it all by spending most of my time drinking. It seemed I had called to God but now I was thanking the devil. It took me some three years after this to find God. However, that experience lived with me many years, and still does unless I turn it over to God and get the **victory**.

From North Africa we went into Sardinia and on to Italy where after a while I got blown up again and spent another three months in hospital. God had His hand on me all the time and after I came to know Him, I knew I had been saved to serve! By this time the RAF realized I was not an asset but a liability. The war was over out there and they sent me home, where I served in the RAF for about another year.

How things had changed in England. People had grown older, my mother had white hair, my little sister was a teenager and as she came in the house I didn't recognize her. Little girls grow into young ladies after four years.

Upon my return, I felt that I should look up the young lady who had been writing to me for the past three years. I think I caught her on the hop because she was doing housework. Anyway she took me to meet all her friends and as far as I was concerned that was it. But God had other plans for our lives together.

The last few months of my Service life was a good time, I travelled England picking up vehicles, driving them from one RAF station to the next, sometimes coming to the docks in Southampton, never dreaming that one day I would live here. Often I stayed overnight in London and I found myself getting to know Margaret more and more and falling in love with her. She was so different from most of the girls I had known. Although she wasn't a Christian as yet, she had very high principles and we soon planned to marry.

I often feel ashamed before God when I think of all the cheating I did in the RAF, often stealing petrol or anything else I could to get money to play cards. I always had a pack of playing cards on me and whenever it was possible I would get into a card school.

I think I spent more time in Harrow with Margaret than I did in camp. We knew all the ways around the red-tape and could fix it for time off. I can hear her dad now saying 'Do you live here or in the RAF?' I think some of her work mates thought the same, as many times I was waiting for her at the factory gate. At that time she was doing war work in one of the local factories; long hours and low pay.

Thank God for his mercy and grace, it's wonderful to know that the blood of Christ covers all our sins. **Praise His Name**.

Like most ex-servicemen I look back with regret that I didn't use the time to improve myself but I had little or no ambition then. The only person that mattered to me was **me**. After all, I had come home again, after many times thinking that I wouldn't. I realise why now. God had plans for my life that I knew nothing about at the time. I just couldn't think that God could do anything for an uneducated country boy. As I have grown older I just marvel at the grace and power of our God. He is indeed a good God.

Chapter 11

Called Into the Kingdom of God

Eventually I left the Services, although they offered us so much to stay in for another five years. I guess all our experience was useful to them, but like most ex-service-men I was discontented with life in the RAF and wanted to get back home to pick up my life again. We had been told of all the good things that awaited us in England but all we found was a war-torn Britain with little or no place for the likes of us. No work, nowhere to live if you wanted to marry and have a family. Many of us felt rebellious and unwanted, but I little realized what excitement God had planned for my life.

For six months I went back to work on Albert's farm. By this time he had made a lot of money whilst I was away fighting the war. I don't think he was too fussy how he made it; his principles were not very high and it seemed to me that money had become his god and I still hated farm work. I am afraid I would never have made a farmer for all the money in the world.

It was during this time that Margaret and I became engaged. The only problem as far as I was concerned was money. I just couldn't save. I smoked very heavily and liked my drink, and I was also hooked on playing cards. I tried so hard, but found that my life was not my own. How true it was that I needed something or someone to help me. I was to learn within a few months that that someone was Jesus.

I was spending the weekend with Margaret. We used to go to the cinema on Sunday afternoons, have a drink and then catch the train home. But on this particular Sunday as we were about to go in for a drink she started to cry, and then told me she had been saved and given her heart to Jesus. I thought she had gone quite mad. I knew she had a sister Joan who I felt was religious, but this was too much for me so I told her to join the Salvation Army. I would buy her a bonnet and a tambourine and I would go to hell. So I walked off and left her standing there.

I didn't return home. I stayed up there and for three days and nights I couldn't get this salvation thing out of my mind. I was taken ill with malaria which I had suffered from for the last two or three years. As I lay in bed all I could think about was calling to God and then thanking the devil during and after my air crash. I made up my mind that I must look into this. If there was a God then He must be able to do something even for me. I needed Him so badly. I was able to get up out of my sick-bed and go off to see Margaret to know more. What a look of surprise she had on her face as she opened the door and there I stood, because I am sure that she thought I had gone out of her life for ever that Sunday evening. How faithful she was in her witness for her new-found Saviour.

We sat down to talk, with me asking all the questions, most of which she had no answer to. But I remember she turned me to 1 John 1:9 *'If we confess our sin, God is faithful to forgive our sins.'* She has told me since that was about the only verse she could remember, but that was all the Holy Spirit needed to show me the way I was to go. So kneeling down at about 9.15 pm on May 25th I prayed something like this: 'If there is a God and I believe there is, and if you sent Jesus to be my Saviour, and I believe you did, then please save me, and by the way God – could you do it now.' At that moment I just knew I had found what I had looked for over the last twenty-odd years. I found a peace and joy like I had never known before; I found **life**!

Of course everything didn't change overnight; as a matter of fact my first church service the following Sunday left me cold, but as we walked away from that church feeling somewhat disappointed, a young couple invited us to their home for coffee. There we found a group of young people from different churches enjoying fellowship and reading the Word. Praying together, they really loved Jesus. It was all so new to us and I just praise God for that group who picked us up and took an interest in us and led us on as well as they knew how. In fact, it wasn't long before they had us out on the streets with them seeking to reach others for Christ.

Eventually we were baptised and married, but it took us some six months or more to fully understand what the Christian life was all about. How faithful our God was during that time and has proved to be over the last forty years or more.

After our marriage, I left the farm and we lived in Harrow. I was able to get a job with the RAF as a driver – about all I could do at that time. As soon as I started God gave me the strength to witness for Him. I knew I had to start at the beginning or it would be too late. I always feel many young people miss so much because they are afraid to fly their colours for Jesus.

Driving for the Service meant I had a lot of time waiting for Officers, and I spent every moment I could reading my New Testament. How new it all was to me. I just loved the book of Romans and I would read it and read it. Often it was just like a personal letter from God to me. Because I got my leg pulled and often asked a lot of questions, most of which I had no answers for, I always replied that I would ask my Pastor. How patient that dear old man was with me and all my questions. I was also asked by the lads if we could study the New Testament in our lunch time. We started at St John, some five or six of us meeting once or twice a week and often it was back to the Pastor for the answer.

I often preach, 'Expect great things from God. Attempt great things for God.'

I believe that sums up our testimony, but having said that, looking back over the last few years, I realise that there is no end to what God can and will do if only we are faithful to Him.

As you will see in my story, I had to learn this over and over again, and I hope I will always be willing and ready to learn.

I would much sooner burn out than rust out. Having said that, I know that our bodies are the temple of the Holy Spirit (1 Corinthians 6:19). Therefore we must look after them and use them for His glory.

Some years afterwards I met a man in a Baptist Church who told me his seeking for God started in those Bible studies. When I met him he was working for God, a born-again Christian. How true the Bible is when it says *'cast your bread upon the waters, for after many days you will find it again'* (Ecclesiastes 11:1).

For two years I studied with correspondence courses, because I always felt that one day God would call me into evangelism. With my lack of education I didn't feel I had much hope but believed in a God of the impossible. In 1948 I joined the Christian Colportage Association going from door to door selling Christian books and Bibles. During this time I learnt so much and I rejoice that I saw folk accept Christ as their Saviour. I also continued my studies by going to London Bible College two evenings a week. I couldn't take any exams because of my lack of education but I grew to love the Word of God more as I came to understand something of it.

After the war things were very difficult for young married couples. We had very little money and there was a housing shortage so we lived with my in-laws. One room up and one room down, sharing the kitchen. We had no bathroom, and an outside loo. But somehow we managed by saving a little and getting our home together.

I now come to the biggest battle of my Christian life. We wanted a child of our own but after many tests on both of us, we were told we could never have any. I always remember visiting one day and a woman came to the door. She had 12 or 13 children. There seemed to be children everywhere and I had the impression she didn't care too much about any of them. She was just letting them run wild. I just fell apart inside of myself. I had to return home and all I could say was 'Why God? We only want one or two.' But once again He gave the victory.

After much discussion and prayer we planned to adopt a child and Peter came into our lives. What a happy event that was. At last we had family of our own. Of course that brought problems regarding accommodation. We were living with an old couple that Margaret was looking after, and we had two rooms. They were a lovely old couple, and had agreed to us having Peter, but just two months after bringing Peter home Margaret became pregnant and we had to leave them with nowhere to go. We went to the Council for accommodation, but as far as they were concerned we had somewhere to live so they couldn't help.

Once again Margaret's parents opened their home to us and we went back to sharing with them.

These were hard times for us both after Andrew was born. We were living in two rooms with two small babies and the strain began to be felt by all. Remember there were no washing machines in the early fifties, and how Margaret managed to do all the washing I don't know. I remember there always seemed to be nappies hanging everywhere.

By this time I had come off door-to-door work because of my health, working in the office of the CCA buying and supplying for the men out in the field of evangelism. After working in the office all day I often had to go to meetings for them to make the work known, returning home quite late.

The next big event in our lives together was that Margaret became pregnant again. This gave us quite a shock; after all, we had been told we could never have children, and here we were about to have number three!

During my lunch time in the office I picked up a Christian magazine and saw an advert for free accommodation. An ex-manse; the rent and rates were free in exchange for cleaning a Baptist Chapel in Wiltshire. I just knew I had to write there and then. When the reply came back I found I knew the Minister to whom I had written. A date was arranged and off I went to Frome to meet him and to look at the house. It wasn't much, but it offered us a home – our very first. We knew God had answered our prayers and I left the CCA and off we went to live in Chapmanslade, a little country village.

Chapmanslade is a village on top of a hill on the borders of Wiltshire and Somerset. The cottage was down a lane next to a Baptist Chapel where they held services on Sunday afternoons.

When we arrived from Harrow we were met by the family next door with cups of tea and sandwiches. We were to spend many happy hours with them in the coming days.

The cottage was old but it was our first real home. Can you imagine how we felt? Two children, another on the way and a home at last. It was a lot of hard work to get it up together but God used it for His glory and young people came to visit us.

I had my own garden again, something I always wanted because I find gardening relaxing, and the country air was so fresh and clean after living in a town. There was a little village shop that sold almost everything we needed. It was not only the local shop but the local 'gossip shop'.

Chapter 12

Called Into Service for God

A few days before we moved, I had a letter from an evangelist called John Hunter asking me if I could help him out during the summer months. This was about June time and he planned a summer tent campaign and needed someone to visit for him during the day. He said he would pay me the same salary I had been receiving, so we moved from Harrow on the Friday. I went to see him on the Saturday and started on the Monday. How God plans it all out for us.

He called it Coronation Year Campaign, and started in Bath in the car park of the cricket ground. I visited Bath during the afternoon and helped with the tent meetings in the evenings. People came to Tent Mission then and most nights were full, with several people coming to know the Lord. Each campaign was fifteen days non-stop. Then we moved on to different places, all the time learning and rejoicing in what God was doing, and often able to lead people to the Lord in their own homes.

The last campaign of the summer was booked for Frome. Again my days were spent in visiting, with John preaching every night. People came in from the villages around and often we had to let the sides of the tent down so that people could hear and see what was going on.

During one of these lovely warm summer evenings we had more people come than ever before. The only problem was, the evangelist didn't arrive! What panic! What would happen now? We sang some hymns and then more hymns and still no evangelist. So I got up and gave my personal testimony and invited people to come to Christ. This was the first time I had ever made an appeal. You can imagine how I felt when some eight or ten people got up and came to the front. I was able to give them a short talk on the Christian life, and that was the start of my life as an evangelist.

Three nights afterwards we were coming to the end of the summer campaigns when three local businessmen asked me if I would work around the villages if they would support me for six months. So I continued to visit every day taking St John's Gospel from door to door. To this day as I pass through some of those villages I can remember contacts I made. I am sure that one day in Glory I shall meet people saved during these days.

By this time Pauline had been born, and how excited we all were to have a little girl. Again I wonder how Margaret managed with all the washing etc. She also had to clean the chapel for Sunday Service that was held in the afternoon. By this time we also had young people coming to our home for Bible study, so life was full, and we were happy serving Jesus together. I was often away in the evenings because I was receiving openings for village missions in the chapels around.

As I write my mind goes to some of the little places we worked in, and I remember people who I met and led to Jesus. Young people who are probably now married with their own families, old people who are now with the Lord. I often wonder what happened to this or that person.

My time with these three men was coming to an end. They told me they couldn't support me indefinitely and why didn't I write to some of the societies who were doing the same work as I was. This I did, and had some interviews, but the answer was always the same – you haven't been to Bible College, you have no education, you will not last, we cannot afford you.

I had meetings booked ahead, a heart for God, and a concern for souls, but I seemed to have come to a dead end. Once again though, we were to prove that our God is able.

Margaret and I spent some time in prayer and after a time we felt God was asking us if our faith was in Him or some society, so we prayed something like this: 'We will look after your business God and leave You to look after ours. We need a living wage weekly and when you stop the supply, we shall know you want us to stop.' In our minds we made Friday the day we needed our keep and left it all with God. He was faithful for the next fifteen years, supplying our daily needs.

During the winter months I started to go to Youth for Christ rallies, giving my testimony in many towns up and down the country. Often I would arrive the month after top name preachers, and I had to learn the truth of 1 Corinthians 1:27–2:5 – the God who calls is the God who empowers, and as Roman 1:16 says, the gospel of Christ is the power of God.

The following summer the farmer who owned the tent asked me to take it over and use it as I felt God would have me use it. A young lad who was good with children and a very good musician came and joined me for the summer. We would hold children's meetings at 6 pm, followed by 7.30 pm rallies. God used us together for the next three years, doing 15-day Missions and taking five Missions each summer. It was hard work because we always tried to visit every house in the village, but also so rewarding as we saw families come to Christ and their lives changed.

Chapter 13

Our God is Able

In my work with Youth for Christ, I was privileged to speak at many of their Saturday Rallies up and down England because in the fifties any town of any size held a Youth for Christ Rally. It all started for me because my very dear friend and brother in Christ, Frank Farley of the NYLC, sent me in his place to Walshall because he had a cold. I arrived at short notice, feeling very nervous and was told what was expected of me, and how counsellors would come forward when I made the appeal. Until then, I had only been working in small meetings, doing my own thing in my own way. Sunday they had me planned in two different churches, and all I can say is how God came in for me, for over twenty young people made a confession of faith that weekend.

But that's not the end of the story. Late on Sunday I received a message from Frank to go to Plymouth. He had contacted Margaret and found out I was free, and before I knew it I was on the train to Plymouth.

Can you imagine how I felt when I arrived at a large church and saw my name up there beside Frank Farley? How much I owe to dear Frank.

I cannot begin to describe to you what God did in my life that week. I wept and prayed that God would enable me and he did. During that Mission I saw a husband and wife come to Christ; both Bachelors of Law, and the local GP and his wife. They became flying doctors in Australia.

God showed me the power of the Gospel, and that it was not only knowing, but proving

> *'It's not by might or by power but by my Spirit said the Lord Almighty.'* (Zechariah 4:6)

I understand what Paul meant in Romans 1:16. I am not ashamed of the gospel, because it is the power of God for the salvation of everyone who believes. Looking back over the years I have seen many come to Christ as the Gospel has been preached. I would love to say that they have all gone on with Jesus. All I can say is that I was faithful in the preaching of the gospel and therefore fulfilled my calling.

Someone once said to me it only takes the Gospel to bring them into faith in Christ, but it takes the Church to lead them into discipleship.

Let me describe what summer tent work was like. First we would always pray about where we should go. When that was decided, the tent would be taken from winter storage ready to be put up with the help of local Christians. Summer always started on Whit Monday, so the tent was put up the Friday before. On Monday we would hold a Bible convention with some well-known Bible teachers, with an afternoon meeting, a picnic tea and then our evening meeting.

Our days would begin with morning prayer and preparation at home, meeting at the tent about 2 pm and then visiting door to door. We always tried to visit every house in the village. At 6 pm Tim would hold a meeting for children and then he would play for my meeting at 7.30 pm. We rarely made open appeals in our meeting, but as one or another came to know the Lord, on the last night or two we would ask them to make an open confession of their new-found faith by coming to the front. I would say that most of them were very willing to do that.

Most of our missions were for fifteen days non-stop and some were for twenty-one days. On many missions I wouldn't get help and had to do it all myself. I wonder how I stood up to it, but 'our God is able.'

Every year for fifteen years we held some five missions each year, where many made confessions of faith. In the winter it was village halls or churches and chapels. I know of no greater thrill than seeing someone come to Jesus and the joy on their faces when they confessed Him.

Whole families would come to the tent and often they all came to the Lord. One family I remember lived in Wiltshire. The three girls came to the tent, but mother always stayed outside until one night I asked her why. She said she was afraid to upset her husband, so I took off to see him while the children's meetings were being held. He was not pleased to see me at all and soon told me so!

He was a very big man and pushed me onto my back on the lawn. I got up and said he was either a fool or a coward. He asked why, so I told him that big as he was, he was afraid to meet God. That was the turning point, and the following night with an air of bravado, he arrived with the family. For some five or six nights he came to the 7.30 meeting, and on the last night of the mission he came forward with his four girls, as he called them. That was in the late fifties. Only this year I had a phone call from him, still in fellowship with God. That was such a joy after all the years of hard work.

The importance of praying where we should go was shown by some wonderful ways in which the Holy Spirit led us to the right place at the right time. I remember Seend village. I had never been there before, but God laid it on my heart, and as I went round the village seeking His will one Monday morning, I learned that only the night before, the chapel people had met, and were going to invite me to come. How God blessed the older people there. Some seven pensioners came to Jesus, as well as a couple who still send me a birthday card. Bert and all his family came to the Lord. Today he is still a local preacher.

Then there was Mear in Wiltshire. I set off not knowing
what God had planned. The first person I met, I asked if
he knew of any Christians. He replied that I was looking
at one! He took me home to meet his wife and I found that
they, with two others, had been praying every week for
God to send someone with the Gospel. We booked the
Town Hall for a fortnight in the winter and every night it
was full. Some thirty people came to Jesus.

I could go on and on. I often asked 'Why me Lord?'
God's reply was, 'Have I not sent you?' When God calls,
God is able.

Over the last few years I have met several people who
were saved in the early sixties, in fact we were on holiday
in Wiltshire and went to the local Baptist Chapel. The
preacher was one who had come to the Lord in the tent,
and in that service we met six others who we had seen
saved and blessed and were still going on with God.

During this time we moved from Chapmanslade to a
small village called Crockerton. We took over a closed
Baptist Chapel. It had not been used for many years so we
had to clean the school room to start a Sunday School.
Margaret ran this and it grew very fast. We also had a
Youth Club, and we would hold special services for
Christmas, Easter and Harvest. Also whenever I was free
I would do a bit of visiting, every year giving Gospel Gem
Calendars to every house. I remember calling on Lord
Bath the next year, and he had it up in his study and
would tell me the text for the day. I believe the Word of
God can also do its own work, if only we are faithful and
seek to distribute it to the people.

The work grew so that we were able to open the chapel,
raise the money to redecorate it, and put lighting and
heating in. The highlight for me was to open the open-air
baptismal pool. What a job. It hadn't been opened for
100 years. I spent two or three days cleaning it out and
filling it up again. On August 5th 1960 (my birthday) we
were baptising seven people, so we wrote to the local

newspaper and we had between 200 and 250 turn out for this event.

It was about this time I felt that I had to see my father and tell him I had forgiven him and that Jesus was willing to do the same for him. So I set off not quite knowing where to look. I started at the Court House in Spalding. They couldn't help because they had no address, but they did say they thought he lived somewhere in Bedfordshire. So off I went to a village Post Office and started by asking if they knew of a Mr North, but with no success. I was about to give up when I was told by a village postman that a Mr North lived down the lane. A woman came to the door when I knocked. I just knew that at last I had found the right place. She showed me where he was working and as I entered the field he came over to me asking me if I was looking for the boss. Then he stopped in his tracks and said 'You are Len.' I cannot express my feeling, except to say after thirty years I felt no bitterness.

He took me to meet the so-called Mrs North, and told me I had a step-sister aged 14. Both said how sorry they were for all the hurt they had caused us and wanted me to keep in touch. My reply was that I had managed for thirty years without him and how could I hurt that fourteen-year-old the way I had been hurt! To cut a long story short, I told him what I had come for – and told him about Jesus and left. I heard a while ago that he had died. I wonder if they ever trusted the Lord? All I can say is I did what I had to.

As time went on I was moving more and more westward and spent a lot of my time away from home, in Somerset and Devon. We did eight missions in North Devon, some with the tent, some in village halls, and we called them North Devon Campaigns. One mission stands out in my mind; as I made the appeal one night, eight people came out and as they stood there I learnt that the youngest was nine and the oldest was ninety. God is no respecter of age or person. How sad that although the young girl had a life to live for Jesus, the old lady had to wait so long before she knew the peace of God in her heart. Those were her own words to me.

Looking back on the Devon Missions, I always recall going to a follow-up rally. The minister who was leading the meeting went on and on about what great work we had done, praising man and not giving God all the glory. I began to get very low in my spirit with all this. Then God said, look out and look up. I looked out at some 100–130 people in that meeting and counted some 30–35 who had come to Christ as a result of the Campaigns. I just needed to praise the Lord and by the time I had to bring the Word I was all fired up. What power came upon us all that night.

I must tell you about an invitation I had to a village in Devon. I was booked for three weeks, during which time I was to preach a week each in the three churches, the Methodist, Congregational and C of E. The first week was well supported by the church people, but no outsiders came in from the village. On the Sunday we were in the manse, with everyone being nice to one another like Christians should, when there came a knock at the door and there stood a young lad who asked to see me.

Going to see what he wanted, he asked me to get on his motor bike which I did, and within five minutes I would have given anything to have got off again, as we went down the lanes at a good 60 mph!

We arrived at a houseboat and walked across a plank and down into the hold, where there about 20–25 young people, smoking and drinking by candlelight. A big lad of about 22 stood up. He must have been 6ft 4inches, and he said, 'Well Preacher, what have you got to say for yourself? You have spent a week preaching to the church folk, what about us?' I felt afraid. After all, no-one knew where I was and I could see myself ending up in the River Torridge. By this time it was about 10.00 pm.

I said, 'if you want to know I will tell you,' and I started from my early days and gave my testimony of God's grace. I went on and on because I felt if I stopped I'd had it! But when I came to a stop, the big lad told me he had just come out of prison and this was a coming-home party. He felt just like I had before I became a Christian. As I was about to leave (by this time it was long passed midnight), I asked if I could pray with them, and asked them to invite Christ into their lives, promising I would hold a meeting just for them in the park the following night.

To cut a long story short, I cancelled all the church meetings, which didn't make me the most popular preacher in town with the Christians, and after many phone calls I was able to get a tent brought down and put up by a Christian from Bristol. I also phoned another evangelist I knew in Cornwall and asked for help. He was free and came over, as well as a Youth Group from Looe, so off we went!

We started at six o'clock for the children. They came in their droves, and I often think of little Willie, who was about 10–11 but had to pop out half-way through the meeting for a smoke. I called him Woodbine Willie; a lovely lad. At 7.30 pm the other evangelist led and preached for older folk, which was not as well attended. Then at 9 o'clock we got ready for the young folk to arrive. To my surprise about 40 odd turned up. There were bikes and motorbikes everywhere.

On their first evening, three of the lads told me they had become Christians the night before on the boat. One had been beaten up by his father as a result. Of the others, one had been sacked from his job and one came from a Christian home.

So many of them didn't know what to expect, and neither did I for that matter. We started to sing 'There is a Green Hill Far Away' and 'Onward, Christian Soldiers'. Most of them knew a few of the words, and you couldn't see across the tent for smoke in the end – but who cared! I didn't. I just wanted to tell them about Jesus. God was there, and for ten nights they came. What sadness we found. Such as one 13-year-old who told me she was having a baby by her grandfather. For several years both

she and her sister had been abused. We left them in the
hands of the law. Then there was the young farm worker
who came to the Lord one week and was killed on his
motorbike the next.

Some two months afterwards, I was asked to call and
see them, and I shall never forget standing outside the
Methodist Church Hall listening to them taking their own
meeting. Still singing the same two hymns, reading the
Word, and praying together. I must confess I stood there
with tears in my eyes. As I entered they greeted me like a
long lost brother. But how sad to hear they had been
asked to move away because they didn't go to church.
This has always been a problem; getting young people to
relate to a church fellowship because all too often they
don't fit in, and sad to say, they were not always
welcomed because of their way of life.

Around this time our Denise came into our lives. Our
little PS I called her, and how the three older ones loved
her. Mum and Dad were so happy to have another little
girl in the family. The only problem was she arrived a
little late to fit in with our plans, because we were moving
house at the time.

The Baptist Church in Hemyock Devon, had been left a
cottage and the minister who was a very dear friend of
ours felt we should buy it. However the cost was £750.00.
Where do you get that kind of money from when you live
by faith? Somehow Rev. Cotton had talked the Council
into giving us a mortgage if we could raise the £50.00
deposit. I remember calling at the manse for coffee on my
way to Cornwall and saying that if I returned with the
£50.00 we would buy it.

It was always my policy to call on converts afterwards if
that was possible. I would often go to the next place early
with that in mind. The very first farm I passed I called in
to see a family with three children. All five members of the
family had been saved during one mission. As I was leaving, the father gave me an envelope. After I left I opened
it, and inside was £25.00. At the very next farm a mother

and daughter had been saved. They called the man of the house, who was not a Christian as far as I knew, and he gave me an envelope saying how his family had changed and he wanted to show his appreciation to me. Yes, you've guessed right. When I opened the envelope, there was £25.00, and within two hours of leaving the manse I had the money. God was proving his faithfulness yet again.

I should have learnt that months before because I was already driving around in a new van that He had supplied during that same year, with trade-in on my old car and with £500.00 that came in on the very day I was to collect it. I had four new ones after that – all provided by God. Praise His Name. God blessed and provided over these fifteen years. We can truly say that God's children will lack no good thing. But in it all and above it all, the greatest miracle of all is the new birth. To see lives changed by the power of God, and the work of the Holy Spirit.

By the late 1960s God showed me I must spend more time with my now growing family. I never seemed to have time at home with them. So we asked God where we should go from here.

As I had travelled I had been offered several pastorates. At this time the churches were quite free to invite anyone whom they felt God was calling, and the fact that I had no Bible college training wasn't that important. After all, I had proved God's calling upon my life for the last fifteen years or so.

I went to several places seeking God's will, having different churches asking me to consider going to them. But in the end I felt God was calling me to Binfield, Berkshire. It was the last place I wanted to go to, but Margaret and I knew it was God's calling. So early in 1964 we arrived at an old run-down manse. They gave us a great welcome and the folk in the fellowship had done their best to make the manse presentable and were waiting for us with cups of tea.

The church was also run down, and I had two village chapels to care for. I don't think anything had changed for years. The salary was small but we knew it was God's place for us.

Most Sundays we had about 10 people attend, and Margaret started a Sunday School. After a while we held Family Services in the mornings but nothing seemed to move. I remember after about six or eight months, I went into my study and said 'That's it, I'm leaving at the end of the year.' I can still hear Margaret saying 'Did God call or not? If you know He did, get up and get on with it. Look to Him and not the people.'

From that time on God blessed us and the work just began to grow. During my visiting I began to meet one and another who had some Christian contact, and several began to come to the Family Services. The children went to Sunday School and Binfield Free Church became known. Within three years you had to come early to get a seat. The offering grew and we were able to make several improvements to the church, but I must confess we didn't see much improvement in the two village chapels. It seemed to me that they just wanted to stay the way they had always been. Sadly, they are both closed now. After I had seen this happen I realised we go forward with God or die a Spiritless death.

Reflecting on these two churches, I see a picture of so many churches and chapels where we have held missions and seen many young folk confess Christ, but the older people would not move over to make room for them. Oh yes they were pleased to see the growth in numbers, but somehow they seemed threatened by the new life shown by these new babies in Christ, and therefore they were not willing to change anything to accommodate them.

I remember one village where we worked for over a month and saw much blessing. I went back a month later to find their congregation had grown from about twenty to over seventy. Yet sad to say in that chapel, there was one dear old soul who had kept the chapel open, and though she had a heart of gold, she also had the spirit of 'As it was in the beginning, is now and forever will remain so.' I am so pleased to be able to say I still hear from some of the converts of that mission today.

As an older man, I know it's not easy to let go and let others get on with the job, but I am so grateful that in my early days there were those that not only made room for me, but gave me all the help and encouragement I needed. I have always believed that the way to encourage new converts is to give them something to do. All too often we feel we must teach, and so we must, but we need to use new converts to make them feel they are being useful in the Kingdom of God.

During the last two years there as the work had grown. I became a pastor and not an evangelist. But the truth is I am an evangelist, and I just couldn't carry on in the church. Having to preach to the same people three or four times a week was just too much. I still had a heart that longed to reach out to the lost. I did this at the odd Youth for Christ Rally but how I missed preaching to the unsaved.

I suppose I was a successful pastor but I was becoming a private failure. I had to learn the hard way that it's not what we do for God that matters, but the relationship we have with God. I found myself in a deep spiritual wilderness which led to me thinking and doing things that were not of the Spirit of God. Oh yes, I was a good organiser, but an awful husband and father. Pride would not let me admit that even to myself.

The church had grown in numbers and we had new buildings built, but somehow I was missing out. This in turn took its toll on my health, so the time came after six years that I had to leave.

How gracious our God is, because although we had nowhere to go, at just the right time He gave us a little cottage in Dorset. Just one up and one down, yet again it proved to be His provision for us. I went to live down there for three weeks to get it ready for us to live in. Then we moved to Bridport with Denise. Peter was in the RAF,

Pauline and Andrew had jobs in Binfield and stayed there for a while, and we had to start a new life.

This, of course, meant that I had to find a job. I wasn't trained for anything but again the opening came up and I went to work in a garage. Margaret became a home help and enjoyed it very much.

For the next eight years it was work and more work as we made the cottage the place we dreamt it could be. We got a grant to help us. I spent hours pulling down walls and building them up again and doing all the things one has to do to modernise an old cottage. Then I had an accident and spent a lot of my time in and out of Weymouth Hospital – some 16 or 17 times in all. Our marriage almost came to an end. During those eight years of our lives, we had little or no spiritual help from anyone. Maybe they wanted to help and I wouldn't let them; I don't know.

All this began to change when Pauline and Ray booked us in to Bible Week. I didn't want to go, and in my mind there was no way I would go, but God had other ideas for us, because He led us to a caravan and took away all our excuses!

I cannot begin to explain my first reactions to these first meetings, I was so mixed up. I had never met people like this. I felt they must be mad, all this singing and dancing, speaking in different tongues, talking of healings. After all, I had always felt this was only in the days of the early Church that things like this happened. Soon I was to learn better.

Chapter 14

A New Life at Sixty

I made up my mind I would just go to the teaching on evangelism. After all, that was where my heart still was because I had never lost the desire to reach the lost, although I was spiritually cold myself. I knew that people outside of Christ needed to hear the Gospel.

The meetings were good and I enjoyed them. After the meeting one morning, the leader called me aside and said, 'You used to be an evangelist didn't you?' My reply was, 'Who told you that?' and to my surprise he answered, 'God!' Now I had not moved in prophecy and had a problem accepting that, but he went on to say that God wanted to use me again and train others in evangelism, and that I would see things like never before.

I must confess that I was a bit sceptical of this, but I went back to Bridport and began to get involved with Youth for Christ again. Within a matter of months, we started a house group in our home. I found that once again I was being used in the salvation of others. What was more important I was walking with God again, as I began to read His Word and seek to serve Him. There is now a Christian Fellowship in Bridport that came out of that house group.

As the time came around for the next Bible Week, we felt we should go again to find out more about these things, so we booked again. It was then that God really took over. We were due to go on the Friday, but the Sunday before, Margaret said that she felt we should go and live in Southampton, find a church fellowship that was moving in the Spirit and maybe God would bless us.

My reaction was, 'Why? I have all I need here.' I was in a business on my own, had a lovely cottage with all I should need for my retirement and I had a house group to run. Anyway, I said that if God sold our cottage by the end of the week then I would go. I didn't want to sell and had no intention of doing so, but I felt my reply would keep her happy and give me a way out of the situation. On the Thursday evening, I picked up the phone and heard someone asking if we wanted to sell, and if so, how much. Now I know that was God because we had told no-one, and the person interested lived some way away, therefore we had to obey God.

We went off to Bible Week and God blessed us because we were now open to His blessing. We met and made many new friends and also people who had been saved in our meetings years before. How great is our God!

Within eight weeks we had sold our cottage, bought a house and moved into Eastleigh, little knowing at that time we had moved to within four hundred yards of where Eastleigh Christian Fellowship met. The week before our move, I found myself praying in tongues, yet I felt that I still had a long way to go, because it is possible to use tongues and miss out on the other eight gifts of the Spirit.

One of the great surprises in going to ECF was the love shown towards us. I had been used to the hand-shake of welcome, but when guys came up to hug me, I wondered just what I had come into. I thank God that since then I have learnt to express my love for my brothers and sisters in the same way.

It took us some six months to settle in, but we were overwhelmed by their love for God and for one another. We soon realised what we had been missing for many years and became involved in the work and witness of the Body of Christ.

After a while I started door-to-door visiting again and how thrilled I was to meet people on their own door-step once more, and to see some of them come to Jesus. Like the husband and wife in their fifties, who as I preached the Gospel both came forward for salvation.

One day on door-to-door, I came across a little girl aged about two. Her foot was turned inwards and she was under the hospital for treatment. I felt her foot straighten as I prayed for her; my first healing miracle! Almost next door lived a lady who had been away from the Lord for some seven years. She came back to the Lord and has since been baptised in the Holy Spirit and is going on with God.

After the wilderness years, it was wonderful to stand before the people again with the Gospel and see God work as folk came to Christ. How true is Joel 2:25,

'I will repay the years the locusts have eaten.'

God has proved this to Margaret and me.

I'm now looking to God to fulfil all the prophecy, and I'm believing God for miracles. I know our God is able, because once again God is taking the impossible and making it possible; I'm learning again the walk of faith and how to step out with God.

The week before Easter 1989, I couldn't sleep and Jesus came to me. I could see Him standing at the foot of my bed so clearly. I have never known it quite like that before. We began to talk to one another and He said to me that from that day for the next two years I was going to see things that I had never seen before. Not being very full of faith I asked for a sign and He gave me five names and told me to stand before the people on Easter Sunday and call them forward for different reasons: two for salvation, one for healing and the other two, a man and his wife, for renewal. I got up and wrote the names down and left them in my heart, telling no-one of this. When I made the call, one by one these people came forward and I knew that God was showing me the start of great things in His name.

Since that day, doors have opened and people have been saved and baptised in the Spirit as I have moved from place to place.

It would be good to name some of the places I have been to but they wouldn't mean much to you. Just to say I started to see folk slain in the spirit after being saved, this was a new experience to me. I don't think I will ever forget the first two; I was just praying for them and down they went. Before, I had always felt that maybe they were pushed, but I can honestly say I have never pushed anyone; in fact I often don't touch them, just reach out in faith to God for the Holy Spirit to do His own work.

About that time we came into contact with Pietro Cressano. He had been saved in Kings Church at Chandlers Ford. About three months afterwards he had a car accident and is now in a wheel-chair. We were privileged to be able to accommodate his family as they came over from Italy to visit him. During his stay here there was always one member of his family over here. We became very close to them during their testing time and I rejoice to say several members of his family have become believers in the Lord Jesus Christ.

I had a call to go to Italy but as I hadn't been in an aeroplane since my crash, I wondered how I would feel. As I was taken to the airport and we took off, I have never known the peace of God quite like it. In fact I asked myself why I wasn't nervous and God replied, 'Because I'm with you.'

Arriving in Italy, I was met at the airport and taken into Turin to stay with some friends who had arranged for me to go. What happened that week would fill a book as I enjoyed hospitality from the Cressano family in their lovely home in Gabiano.

The first two days I spent finding my way around and on the Sunday we went to an Evangelical Church in the next village. It was a lovely service; what I could understand of it. At lunch time we met as a family and broke bread together and afterwards we went into Turin to a Pentecostal Church. Around 60–65 people were there and they asked me to give the Word. Now I have only spoken through an interpreter once before and this guy wasn't too good on his English, but we got by for about fifteen minutes. I then made an appeal and one man and a ninety-four year old lady came forward. How wonderful it was to see her face as Jesus came into her life. I prayed for two others for healing and then the service ended, or so it seemed as people began to leave. Then a woman started to cry to God for mercy and began to praise God in tongues. I could understand every word she said. I had never known this before and it blessed me.

During this time people were coming back in and many more began to cry for mercy, asking for more of Jesus. I moved amongst some fifteen to twenty of them, praying with them, and as I prayed, one after another they began to praise God. I was beginning to see the miracles God had promised. In all my life I have never known the Holy Spirit to move like that before.

For the next few days of my stay in Italy it was wonderful to be able to talk to folk about Jesus. It seems to me that the people of Italy are hungry for God and I pray that some of us will be sent back to tell them of Him.

My diary records the continued fulfilling of God's prophecy for me

October 1989 – I have just returned from a mission outreach in Bridport, my first for about fifteen years. How good it was to take a team of ten of us working with Bridport Christian Fellowship, seeing young men getting saved and all ages getting baptised in the Holy Spirit. During the eight days down there, some eighteen came to the front. Praise our God.

November 1989 – I have just returned from my second visit to Italy. It was good to see some Christian Fellowships now starting up in the North of Italy and on the

Sunday they held a joint celebration. There were some seventy-five to eighty present and again I was asked to give the Word. After two hours of worship I didn't find it very easy but once again God was able and afterwards about ten people came forward for prayer, three getting baptised in the Holy Spirit and many others blessed.

What a year 1989 has been for me, seeing real blessing in God and moving of His power wherever I have been. I wonder what the new year holds for us. I look forward to it with a spirit of anticipation and excitement, praying for a great out-pouring of God's Holy Spirit.

As we start the new year, I have been asked to head the evangelism team of four young folk, seeking to teach and train them in evangelism. Again I know this is the answer to the prophecy given me some seven years ago at Bible Week. It seems ages ago but how faithful is our God.

March 1990 – Spent another five days in Italy and how privileged I have been to see God move again in signs and wonders. After arriving at the Cressano home, I found people coming to their home asking more about God and the movement or the Holy Spirit. At their house group, God gave me words of knowledge for two people. One of them came to the Lord, got baptised in the Holy Spirit and healed at the same time. Denise came with me this time and we were able to minister to them. One lady had been a nun for fourteen years and had only just found real blessing.

The most exciting thing was on the Sunday evening. About ninety people crowded into a hall and I brought the Word to them. About twenty-five came forward for prayer, some in repentance and faith in Christ, others for baptism of the Holy Spirit and others for healing. One woman limped in and went out dancing. I found myself prophesying over people and in one case having to stop the meeting to cast out a demon from a woman. What joy showed on her face as the Holy Spirit took His rightful place.

I never thought I would be so privileged in my

mid-sixties to see such signs and wonders following my preaching. Truly we have a God of miracles.

I have just returned from Italy again. What a busy and yet blessed time. I had five meetings in six days, and it was good to meet people who had been blessed during my previous visits still going on with God. One of my great joys was to attend an open-air baptismal service in the local river and see people who had previously been bound by tradition and religion, coming out into the freedom found in Christ. One young lady with tears running down her face said to me, 'How wonderful to be free in Christ.'

I was also able to talk to one couple who I had prophesied over last time. They had been married for six years and their hearts desire was to have children. My prophecy was that she would be pregnant by the end of the year. She is now expecting a baby later in the year. I honestly believe it was her accepting by faith the prophecy as the Word of God to them, and I give God all the glory.

I am amazed at what God is doing in Italy, but I shouldn't be, because God told me I should see signs and wonders in my old age, and I was sixty-eight yesterday. I just look forward to all He is doing.

It is also exciting to come back home and still see folks saved and blessed in my beloved England, I believe revival is coming soon. Please God may I live to see it.

November 1990 – I went to Italy again for eight days. How good it is to enjoy fellowship with the dear folk over there. I am amazed at the spiritual growth of some of them. How I long to be able to communicate more with them, yet it's wonderful how much God undertakes for us.

I am still hoping and longing for that day when our dear Pietro is up and walking. We spend many hours talking and praying and it's wonderful to see him grow in Jesus. As a family they need our prayers so badly.

April 1991 – What joy to fly out to Italy again this month and this time have Margaret share the trip with me. It was the first time she had been up in a plane. We enjoyed a lovely trip together and spent many happy hours in Gabiano with the Cressano family.

One great joy to me was to hold little Samuel in my arms. I couldn't believe that God had brought a miracle in their lives so soon.

God has told me to go on praying for revival in this land of ours. Somehow I feel we are missing what God is longing to do. As I look back over the years I see times when I believe God was waiting to bless us as a nation. I think of the Billy Graham campaigns in the 1950s and 60s; people were willing and ready to tell about salvation and blessing, and we saw much blessing.

When the Charismatic Movement came, it brought a great move of the Holy Spirit. The gifts were being used and signs and wonders were manifested. It seems to me sometimes that many leaders are setting up their own little kingdom and there is not the unity between the different groups that will allow the Holy Spirit to move in England in the same freedom as was seen in the early days.

This may sound like a criticism of the leadership, but it is not meant to be. It is only an observation of one who for the last forty years has hoped and longed for revival in our land.

You hear much of what God is doing around the world and we all rejoice in that, but my heart is still longing for the same Holy Spirit to move in power in this land of ours.

I honestly believe that when He does He will by-pass the establishment and organisations we have built. I wonder how the church would handle revival? I just hope they have a different attitude towards it than they have to evangelism. I have been told for the last forty years by many, that the church isn't ready for evangelism. I wonder if it is ready for revival?

I come to a close with great expectations of all that God is going to do in spite of our human failure. I know He is going to move in power; whether I shall be around to see it happen only He knows, but how my heart longs to be a part of it. **Please God, do it now!**

1992 – We go forward knowing we have a God who is still faithful and His blessings are new every morning, Praise His Name.

I am planning to go to Italy again in May of 1993, praying about setting up a church in Gabiano. There are already some twelve to fifteen born-again Christians there, but they do need to get together for fellowship.

Margaret has been able to join me on my trip to Italy. Once again we saw the hand of God on our visit, taking over meetings and seeing some thirty-five to forty people come forward for prayer, both for salvation and baptism of the Holy Spirit. It was also wonderful to see the growth in the new Christians from previous visits.

In one meeting as I sat waiting to talk, the Lord spoke to me reminding me of the time I spent in Italy during the war, when I was out there to kill or to be killed, and now here I am in my 70th year going out to bring life in Christ. What a change has taken place in my heart and life! Please God, go on using me to bring life to many others.

May 1993 – Been to Italy again for ten days, during which time I was able to minister at eight different meetings and once again see the power of the Holy Spirit at work, counselling over sixty people for one spiritual need or another.

Each time I think this must be my last visit because I find I get so tired. After all, I have just had my 71st birthday. Yet it is good to know that our lives are in His hands and we never know what exciting adventures lie around the corner. After all, I would sooner burn out than rust out.

1995 – I am now 73 years old. I went to Italy again last year for my ninth visit. I took one young fellow from our church with me and enjoyed his fellowship and support as we worked together. We had eight meetings in 10 days. It was a revelation to him to see the Holy Spirit at work.

This year in April I went alone for a week, and I briefly share some highlights of this visit as I ask for your prayer for that country.

At one gathering of some 300 people, I spoke on the Holy Spirit, and He came to us in power. Some 30 people were slain in the Spirit. I also met people who have been blessed and healed during previous visits.

Over the weekend I met with the Christians in Gabiano for prayer and breaking of bread. The following day I was planning to leave, when I was asked to go to a village nearby to pray for a little boy who had no eyes. He was about four years old I think. When I arrived there was a lot of talking which I couldn't understand so I started to pray in tongues. Within about half an hour the boy came to me and I laid hands over the lad and continued to pray. I felt so full of faith that I fully expected to see eyes in the sockets. It didn't happen then, but I did what I had to do and I can leave it with Father, for He always knows best.

Upon my return to the house, the Mayor of the town was waiting to see me and took me to a restaurant saying, 'I expect you are wondering why I have asked you here.' Of course I was curious, but I soon found that he was also. His first question was, 'What do you believe, Len?' Of course, I was soon telling him of Jesus. I believe that man is not far from the Kingdom.

In writing this book my purpose has been two-fold, one to give glory to God for His faithfulness, and then to encourage you to step out in faith just where you are, knowing that **'Our God is able'**.

God bless you.

If you would like more information about this ministry, please contact Len North at:

20 Selwyn Gardens
Boyatt Wood
Eastleigh
Hants SO5 4PX